Still Water Carving Light

Still Water Carving Light

poems

✎

PEGGY SHUMAKER

Red Hen Press | Pasadena, CA

Book design by Mark E. Cull

Library of Congress Cataloging-in-Publication Data

Names: Shumaker, Peggy, 1952– author.
Title: Still Water Carving Light: poems / Peggy Shumaker.
Description: First edition. | Pasadena, CA: Red Hen Press, 2025.
Identifiers: LCCN 2024007360 (print) | LCCN 2024007361 (ebook) | ISBN
  9781636281681 (paperback) | ISBN 9781636281698 (e-book)
Subjects: LCGFT: Poetry.
Classification: LCC PS3569.H778 S75 2025 (print) | LCC PS3569.H778
  (ebook) | DDC 811/.54—dc23/eng/20240301
LC record available at https://lccn.loc.gov/2024007360
LC ebook record available at https://lccn.loc.gov/2024007361

The National Endowment for the Arts, the Los Angeles County Arts Commission, the Ahmanson Foundation, the Dwight Stuart Youth Fund, the Max Factor Family Foundation, the Pasadena Tournament of Roses Foundation, the Pasadena Arts & Culture Commission and the City of Pasadena Cultural Affairs Division, the City of Los Angeles Department of Cultural Affairs, the Audrey & Sydney Irmas Charitable Foundation, the Meta & George Rosenberg Foundation, the Albert and Elaine Borchard Foundation, the Adams Family Foundation, Amazon Literary Partnership, the Sam Francis Foundation, and the Mara W. Breech Foundation partially support Red Hen Press.

First Edition
Published by Red Hen Press
www.redhen.org

ACKNOWLEDGMENTS

Grateful thanks to the editors and publishers who first welcomed this work:

Alaska Quarterly Review: "Came a Sickness," "Do Not Resuscitate"; *Ascent*: "The Rule You Do Not Break," "The Moon Shines Equally"; *Atlanta Review*: "Hospice as Muse"; *Black Earth Institute Blog*: "Came a Sickness"; *Bosque*: "A Day of Gifts"; *Brevity*: "Zuill Bailey and a 1693 Matteo Goffriller Cello"; *Connotations Press*: "Alive"; *Hobble Creek Review*: "A Barlow Pocketknife and the Concept of Perfection"; *Cutthroat 18, 2023*: "A Day of Gifts," "First," "Waking, Kona"; *Ruminate Magazine*: "Gifts We Cannot Keep"; *Sweet, a Literary Confection*: "Autopsy Report"; *Terrain.org. Letters to America* anthology: "Red Sky"; *Watershed Review*: "A Tiny Infinity," "Eating from the Carver's Hand."

for Joe, always

CONTENTS

I

Month of Thursdays   15

The Moon Shines Equally   17

First   18

The Crossing   20

A Day of Gifts   21

Waking, Kona   26

Moss   27

Two Brain-Injured Women Trundle Downhill   28

Hospice as Muse   30

A Barlow Pocketknife and the Concept of Perfection   32

Morning Ritual—V-10   34

Edges   35

Duty   37

Critical Care   40

A Tiny Infinity   41

Predawn Ritual   42

Seasons, Many More than Four   44

Lamination   46

Rehearsal   47

Do Not Resuscitate   50

Caregiving   52

You Let Me Be   53

Lunar Eclipse   54

II

Came a Sickness   57

Autopsy Report   60

Desert Where Once Was Ocean   63

The Rule You Do Not Break   64

Gila Monster   65

Give and Take   68

Red Sky   69

Saguaro, Hardship   72

History   74

Words in Every Cell   76

Accompanied   77

Dancing With Aziz   80

Electricity   82

Attending to the World   84

Until Now   86

Kintsukuroi: Each Day   87

Beyond   90

Gifts We Cannot Keep   91

Long Married   94

Traveling Beside Water   96

Questions Without Answers   97

Following the Grain   99

A Boy I Know   100

Zuill Bailey and a 1693 Matteo Goffriller Cello   102

Eating From the Carver's Hand   104

Gates of the Arctic   105

Alive   108

Still Water Carving Light

I

I'm disappearing . . .

I want to disappear.

—Joe Usibelli

MONTH OF THURSDAYS

Thursday the thoracic surgeon
split your sternum,
cut away an artery
feeding your chest wall,
stitched it to the starving
part of your heart.
Thursday the critical care
nurse named Brian
gave us straight answers.
Thursday
in rehab
the chipper aide
marking heart monitors said,
"Everyone else warm up.
You sit down."
Straight into a cloth-walled
cubicle, where paddles
shocked your mush-walled heart.
On Thursday I could not stop
staring
at the surgeon's hands.
Sent away that Thursday,
we propped
you up, foam wedges,
the spongy
Extended Stay
bed. We prowled
motel halls all Thursday,
looked forward to Thursday
at home, bathing with Betasept
one long stitch

whipping up your chest,
echoing wires
binding your breastbone.
Unsettled, the Thursday
you hugged to your chest
that heart-shaped pillow.
Is any of us anatomically correct?
Thursday, far thunder,
you did not go under.

THE MOON SHINES EQUALLY

It's not a bad night for the moon.
The moon has a place to live.
Nobody took its kids away.
The moon doesn't skip meals
so its kids can eat.

The moon put itself through college.
Nobody can take that away.
If it wanted, the moon could
get a second mortgage.
The moon's daughters
are not addicts, its sons
not in prison.

The moon watches
a new hatch of rattlesnakes.
Moonlit, they rise
from cold earth
hated
though they do not know

they are hated. Like us
they want the best they can
to live. The moon promises them
no protection. It gives what it has—
secondhand wound-cleansing
light full of longing.

FIRST

Because, my beloved,
    I have no idea
        where you start and I begin

because the ocean,
    like all of us, spits out
        what it cannot swallow

because I admit
    I am not responsible
        for the whole truth

because tenderly I once scrawled
    with a curry comb
        on a dust-cloaked mare my secret

because my cracked shoulder
    reminds me
        of all I cannot reach

because already we are fossils,
    my love, waiting
        for the right eye

because my wrists
    shoot lightning
        cut my breath

because I cannot
    turn a doorknob, cannot
        enter or leave

because, my love, you will die
first or I will
die first.

THE CROSSING

We set off from Whidbey Island, round Cape Flattery, then head down the coast to San Francisco. Incoming waves rollick us the whole way, so my choice is to be flattened by Marezine or to hang out at the rail so I can heave at will.

West toward Kona, we motor under the Golden Gate Bridge, our lives afloat on life-giving, life-taking water. Hours out, we reach that unearthly spot where land is nowhere. Wide blue all around. Our boat seemed large when we could still see shore.

New appreciation, then, for mariners who navigated by currents and stars, shell maps, observation, intuition. We have GPS, charts, weather reports, radios, depth sounders—and still our passage feels precarious.

For half a day, a mother humpback and her calf keep us company, rolling alongside, playing in our wake. Peaceful, this liquid world. For this moment.

Escaping big teeth, flying fish do in fact fly—up out of saltwater, onto the deck. They lie there, stunned. We toss them back, aiming for better deaths than desiccation.

That primal mix of fear and elation—swells building. Following seas— we climb hard at six knots up a green wall of water, crest it, then speed surf down the other side. Thrill ride—go ahead, see what's inside you.

How long would help take to reach us? Longer for sure than watching both hulls of this catamaran tilt, then slip with grace beneath the surface. Life rafts, life vests, life rings, life lines. We think ahead, we humans. And still we launch into the unknown. Open water, the blank page.

A DAY OF GIFTS

Flesh traveling
away from the bone,
each bone its own
precise ache,
reminder of what once

we did without thinking,
thinking now of delirious
hardships we came through
together, what we've made
of our dwindling lives

glorious, cutthroat
morning cribbage,
shampooing one another,
a walk with one person
on foot, one in a jazzy red chair.

Twenty years married,
late in life married,
we witness in one another
sweet softening, sweet
slowing / agony

Caresses around CPAP masks,
we touch one another

with tenderness
reserved for skin

so thin a glance
can bruise it,

skin barely
shielding

blood from air,
skin cool

but not yet
cold.

Outside our window,
a wide swath of willow

zips cross-river,
leaves flickering

green/silver/green
the mouth

holding the branch
the teeth beneath

sleek fur
hidden

so we take on faith
the paddle tail,

bright-eyed
river neighbor

mending her lodge
newly open

after
hard winter.

There will come a day
not too far off

when we won't be
the ones at the window

hand in hand.
In the world then

a new kind of loneliness
exactly the shape

of one beloved
beyond reach.

When we met
we were ready

to make room
to make love

to make lives
shaped exactly

to fit we two
together

and now
our bodies

dosed and probed
braced and worn

our marvelous
aged bodies

take their sweet time
getting where

they have to
(no exceptions) go.

WAKING, KONA

Stars above the skylight
draw near. Barely
light enough
to see your lip
tremble in sleep,
your dream
that far land where
no scars yet
touch right knee, left knee,
shoulder, heart, spine.
Rerouted, your steady thrum
bass line for mourning
doves mating. Mynahs,
finches, glazed
honeycreepers call.
The neighbor's rooster
never crows at dawn.
Wild turkeys, annoyed,
rustle avocado rubble.
Your breath quiet
as yellowlegs flitting
among mangoes,
skittish as swallows
swooping into a new day,
you, nearly gone.

MOSS

Moss doesn't cry
out in the night moss

gathers itself in tiny stars
pale echoes

turn the corner
into the dialysis room

where blood
of my beloved

weaves through
tubes and filters

then returns to him
clean

fresh moss
over lava rock

TWO BRAIN-INJURED WOMEN
TRUNDLE DOWNHILL

for Linda Hogan

On Kona side two brain-injured women
trundle downhill toward the ocean then scrunch
onto loose lava rock and leaf litter

under a massive mango
sheltering dozens of feral
red-crowned parrots.

Among shards of a'a' rests
one downed nest the size
of arthritic cupped hands,

one woven orb
lush as a husked coconut.
No entry we can see

till we turn it twice, again,
then notice a down-lined tunnel
burrowing farther than we can spy.

Within the shelter of arcing
branches, we bend for rose-gold fruits
fallen not long enough ago

so saffron finches, yellow-billed
cardinals, Japanese white eyes
might feast. We pick up

mangoes heavy with juice
but not yet gnawed by francolin or pheasant,
by mongoose, mynah, ants, wild pig.

Two sacks we bring back—
one half full of warm mangoes
deliciously bruised, one sheltering

homes so light
the slightest breeze
skimmed them out of leaves onto pumice.

Sea breezes refresh us,
two puffed out women pausing
on the uphill, so much of our minds

fallen, broken.
What's left
twice alive,

ready
on the slightest breath
to rustle, then fly.

HOSPICE AS MUSE

i.m. Pat Kwatchka

In the summer of rain every day and no wildfires
the river rises so high

beavers swim
only when pink light

rinses their water-
slicked heads,

heads at the point
of each trailing vee

pointed
as any intention.

What is her intention
today, friend

whose lacy
bones collapse, friend

trusting what's left to her
to people who will not test her,

people who honor
what we can never know.

I think today of hours
we squandered (committees,

budgets, justifying
what we'd built)

and hope that most
of those days she rebelled

alive in her private thoughts,
pondering nuances of a phrase

in Choctaw, savoring flavors
of sun-warmed peach,

breathing the aroma
of her beloved

folding her long bones
toward his torso.

Or those nights they fought
like wolverines

black gums framing
fangs they'd kept haloed

in silver fur around their faces,
fangs so private

only those we love
get to see them,

fangs invisible
when into willow and alder

crowding the riverbank
we disappear.

A BARLOW POCKETKNIFE
AND THE CONCEPT OF PERFECTION

i.m. Bill Kloefkorn

To this day, I'm not sure how
you accomplished it, whittling away
on a wienie-roasting stick

out back at Cedar Breaks.
Kept sharp, your good Barlow
(worthy for showing off,

though you hardly ever did
more than three or four times)
sliced right past the nuance

you intended, missed the point
entirely and whittled instead
below the rolled-up sleeve

of your oft-washed
and therefore soft
blue work shirt

this living flesh—sparsely haired
tender underside
of your forearm.

One muscle twitched.
As if in contemplation
of this particular bleeding

instance of life's many and
inexhaustible mysteries,
you regarded what spurted

from your insulted artery—
rhythmic whoosh whoosh whoosh
of some ratchety old sprinkler set off.

Hope it was clean, that green
dishtowel grabbed and pressed hard
to keep the better part of your V8 juice

sloshing inside you.
After the trip to get stitches
after the offer of pills

to slice the edge off
pain left behind
by your very effective bid

for every bit of our attention,
pain any unbiased onlooker
might easily describe as "self-inflicted,"

in dawdling twilight
you lingered outside,
hiked after supper

up the back slope,
hunted another handful of promise—
sticks just about almost all right,

and got started whittling.

MORNING RITUAL—V-10

Into a small glass, a splash
of vinegar, rice wine or apple cider,
whatever's handy.

Then a half-squeeze of light
agave, twelve shakes
of Trappey's Original

Louisiana Hot Sauce.
Fill almost to the brim
with shaken V-8, then

balance the glass
on the curved seat
of the walker

and head out with care
toward the sumptuous
dining room of another day.

EDGES

Hard edge after hard edge,
your retired kidneys, your lungs
swamped, your generous
scarred heart enlarged
by leaning so long into love,
heart flight, heart wild,
heart chop, heart skitter,

hard edges, sharp armrests,
a few bewildered moments
half resting, me bent
in the fake leather
hospital chair,

the woman supervising
your blood, my beloved,
keeps score, filters
midnight. A different woman
wants blood fresh
from an untapped patch—
flips sunrise into our eyes
long before sky lifts
toward day, so

on the sharp edge of
that wee hour you reach
for every lead
plastered to your chest,
rip free
a chaos of beeps alarmed
at your audacity. You demand
a ride, right now,
HOME.

I groan. I cry. I talk
you down.

In four hours
I will try
to make complete
sentences
as I listen
to the expert
who knows
that the edges of
my bones, sharp lace,
may melt from meds
that give the best argument
against another patch
of cells gone rogue,
cells so fierce to live
they edge out
my worn down
dependable
stained shirt
with a rip
self.

DUTY

Whether we accept it or not, volunteer
or are pressed into service, any grownup
recognizes what simply must be done:

the children of addicts must
have shelter, food, stories, and
who's to provide them, who's to swoop in

and willingly give them a home even if
that home strains the lives of boys
who already live there, strains the marriage

of overwhelmed parents,
outnumbered,
dutiful and exhausted,

wiped out like a man whose blood
for four and a half hours
three times a week leaves

his body, travels tubes and filters
and returns cleansed
through his fistula, that vein

whose duty expanded
when the artery sewn into it
stretched it beyond what it thought it could do

and now ripe target
it hosts two large-gauge needles,
one to remove blood

and one to return it,
life-sustaining,
letting the nine-year-old

in her wheelchair
crush more sparkly candy,
letting Paul with his high-tech

titanium leg
walk a few more miles,
letting Joe feel on his face

just before sundown
a welcome moist breeze
fragrant after soft rain

Joe whose duty now
is to do
as much as he can in this world

and then to cultivate
the grace to accept help
he wishes he didn't need

but does in fact need, help given
with love sometimes clumsy
sometimes joyous, love

that notices before need arises
that need will arise
as surely as breath,

as gentle
as breath, as difficult
and hard-won as breath.

CRITICAL CARE

Inside my beloved
tiny beings, mysterious.

A sky full
of cherry blossoms.

A TINY INFINITY

His hands in her hair, her hands
in his, morning in the shower
they share. His hands cup
foam, easing suds

away from her ears,
her belly soap-slick
against his. Their eyes
close under water

warm enough to
cover the mirror.
Rinsed, she steps out,
her footprint dark

on the mat.
Finest moment
of the day—
soft swipe

of fresh cotton plush,
sequins he collects
from the intimate arc
of her back.

PREDAWN RITUAL

After browned mashed potato patty and egg,
a game of Karma.
Wash faces, brush teeth.

Lidocaine ointment squeezed
over his fistula, Press and Seal
over that, then slip the sleeve

of polar fleece over
the wrapped arm.
Six breadsticks and two

Babybel cheeses.
Snack enough
while the machine

pulls from his body fresh blood
cleans it, pulls excess fluid
from his system.

So cold. Everyone in the chairs
feels chilled, their blood
traveling beyond them

and back, restored
to them, reclaimed
through the second needle.

When the tech pulls
the points out of his skin,
he holds pressure

on wads of gauze.
What do they dream,
the many who doze

four hours three times
a week? How it wells up
fast as tears,

deep deep deep
gratitude
for these machines,

these people,
for the great gift
of life with my beloved

long after his kidneys
say sayonara, his
kidneys that just can't

keep up.

SEASONS, MANY MORE THAN FOUR

Season of blue light
    on unshadowed snow

Season of kids with no coats
    at the bus stop

Season of arteries replumbed

Season of willow rising red

Season of snow sifting down
    steadily in May

Season of titanium knees

Season of reaching into earth
    cold and crumbling

Season of vertebrae clipped, fused,
    packed with bone morphogenetic protein

Season of wildfire leaping
    river and road

Season of geese, cranes, swans, ducks
    departing

Season of general anesthetic

Season of ice stretching
    to cover the river

Season of wood frogs
    frozen solid

Season of healing, season of pain
    easing

Season of moose stew simmering

Season of sutures clipped and pulled

Season of coal smoldering underground

Season of salmon longer
    than the freezer is wide

Season of blood risen,
    purple and black

Season of cranes, geese, ducks, swans
    arriving

Season of wood frogs
    sun-revived, again alive

LAMINATION

On the premise that this paper
signed and witnessed

will need to last
the many many years

I want with my beloved,
I coat the orange sheet

in plastic
impervious to flood,

wiped clear of virus,
and secure it

as instructed
to the door

that leads
to berries,

eggs, milk,
canned peaches

chilled and ready
when we are.

REHEARSAL

Away, I call
Home, early morning

And you do not
Answer. Crazy, I fear

You're too weak
To reach

The phone, your CPAP
Gave out

In a power surge,
You gasped

A few last gasps,
You're still alive

Just barely
Maybe

But no way
Can I get

To you in time.
I go over

The million
More likely

Reasons
You're not picking up,

Set them aside
One by one

As if I were
Spelling out

With red
Gumdrops

Your name
On your next birthday cake.

Never in my wildest
Hallucination

Do I tuck you into your ripped
Recliner, buzzing through

A full season
Of *Torchwood*, a series

You know I'd scorn,
Thoughtfully

Staying up
With the aurora and

The waning moon
Then sleeping through

The ringtone
You set for me alone.

Chances are
I will live

Longer than you.
I imagine it,

Your reaching for me,
Our bodies glad again,

New again, awake
Together

Unaware
This is our last time.

DO NOT RESUSCITATE

You weren't afraid, you say,
when you put pen to paper

to instruct those who might
restart your stopped heart

not to,
no,

not afraid.
More calm,

this danger-orange form
making clear

to ones who
know nothing

of you, clear too
to those who

love you well
that you're mindful

that your time
breathing easy

on this earth
is short, your plenty

mostly spent—
six children, ten grandchildren,

great love, piloting
your amphibious

Widgeon, landing
on water, wild and remote, or

off a tiny island
in Fiji,

night diving
to watch soft corals

open their polyps, millions
of mouths

filled with want,
blue ribbon eels coughing,

that considerable current
pulling us

and you
dream flying

letting it take you.

CAREGIVING

On the top rung
of a rickety ladder,
reaching. Soft soil shifts.

YOU LET ME BE

Learning to live in a world
without you
the hardest part
is probably yet to come.

Without you,
who can I be?
Probably, yet to come,
a person I don't recognize.

Who can I be?
Have you taken with you
the self I recognize?
I will never again be

the self you've taken with you.
The hardest part
will always be
learning to live in this world without you.

LUNAR ECLIPSE

Nearly silent
glide of glass doors,
full moon

in earth's shadow.
Nearly silent,
a drip caught

on the great owl's tongue,
owl we don't see
'til we've passed.

With great and nearly silent
dignity it gathers
huge power whooshing softly

lifting low into rare light
lifting level
with my heart

diminishing exquisitely
moon, owl,
heart, silent.

II

Isn't the creative life about folding clothes while crying?

—Fleda Brown

CAME A SICKNESS

The people were used to dying
one at a time

Then came a sickness
upon the land,
came a sickness
to every nation

Came a sickness that killed

the already ill,
killed those who had not known
sickness, killed the generous
who cared for the dying,

killed those who took great care,
killed the careless,
killed those who embraced
worship, killed
those who touched
no God.

The people were used to grieving
by gathering

gathering the goodness each person
brought to the world

Left bereft
we masked ourselves

So many at once,

gone

gone without touching
without goodbye

without rites
perfected
over centuries

Came more sickness

of mind—
scams, lies,
the constant deliberate
epidemic of lies

Came fine minds
crafting vaccines,

came for the lucky
recovery

Came brown blue hazel green
eyes above cloth
seeking other eyes

Came deep grief
opening rituals
we'd never touched

Breathe out, breathe in
this air we share

Each breath
a blessing

each breath
a prayer

AUTOPSY REPORT

My mother's brain weighed 1420 grams.

No discernible measure for the gravity of her mind.

Her thoughts, heavy enough to crush her.

Cyanotic nail beds. General clubbing of the ends of her lungs' alveolar septa. That means her tiny air spaces had real trouble exchanging gases with nearby webs of well-meaning capillaries.

Bronchioles dilated and somewhat tortuous. Somewhat? Can the inability to gasp breath be anything but tortuous?

S. Bennett, M.D.; T. Foreman, M.D.; and H. G. Harrison, M.D. mucked around inside her body, a body consistent with her stated age of thirty-five years. They noted an unhealed incision sutured shut, from the previous day's tracheostomy.

The larger bronchi were filled with whorls of blue-pink stains.

She kept a humpbacked chest in her bedroom filled to the brim with cutout pattern pieces for clothes she intended to sew for us, clothes in sizes we'd long outgrown. Brown tissue straight-pinned to cloth.

Whenever we asked her what something meant, she made us look it up. Mean. She knew, so why didn't she tell us? "Yeah, I'm the meanest mother in the whole world," she deadpanned. Not until years after she was gone did it occur to me that perhaps most of the time she didn't have any answers.

Her pancreas, patchy recent hemorrhage. Her brain, perivascular hemorrhage. She could no longer contain what she needed to keep herself alive.

Vodka bottles in the rag bag, not really hidden. Her liver weighed 1550 grams, with a marked cloudy swelling.

The inner lining of her uterus, worn after four kids and two miscarriages, had broken through the muscle wall. That uterus, I lived there once, her first tenant. On the day she died, a proliferation of cells lived within her, though she may not have known it. We carry so much that we don't perceive, that we can't acknowledge.

Inflammation, chronic. Her temper inflamed almost always. Her intellect, neglected, feverish and throbbing. Edema, swollen responses.

The autopsy lists as her address 5750 T Street, Tucson, Arizona, a place I've never been, never heard of. This appears accurate. She left us.

She traveled so far nobody could reach her. Even in the same room, nobody could reach her.

The postmortem took place on February 2, 1969, the day my mother died. My uncle Kris handed the report to me more than fifty years later. The envelope was addressed to his parents, my grandparents. I had no idea that another uncle, long dead now, had signed papers for an autopsy, no idea that my grandmother had insisted, certain that my mother had not received proper care.

I would bet good money that my grandfather waved the report away, wouldn't read it. His only daughter, dead. Already that was too much. He could not bear images of her body butchered. But my grandmother, who ran the medical records department at a San Diego hospital, would have parsed it, understanding nuances of each Latinate phrase, knowing what was documented and what was left out, combing each detail for answers. My mother, her firstborn. That report left my grandmother alone with *why*.

Grief, a galaxy, endless light from long-dead stars.

My mother's right lung weighed 330 grams, her left 250 grams. Patchy, purple, collapsed, atelectatic.

Diagnosis: bronchiectasis with acute inflammation; chronic and acute obstructive bronchial disease.

So yes, we knew about it. Her illness formed our childhood, the cupboard of steroids, the lunch money can, the pills she swallowed by the handful, the inhalers, the terrible season of blooming palo verde trees. That night neighbors broke her window with a brick so paramedics could get to her.

So much more we did not know, will never know.

Probable cause of death: status asthmaticus, severe asthma unresponsive to repeated courses of inhaled albuterol, nebulizer treatments, subcutaneous epinephrine. Beta-agonists, chemicals intended to ease open tightened airways, medicines intended to relax panicked muscles, to open closed paths for breath.

My mother's wheezing was terrifying. She'd press a fist between her breasts and bend forward, a tiny whistle of air trying to escape her or trying to get in. As a small child, I scooted close beside her in the car as she drove blue-lipped to St. Joe's, aiming for the huge red letters EMERGENCY. I steered when she passed out.

Pupils equal, but moderately dilated. Her irises, like mine, brown.

My mother's heart weighed 330 grams. The cusps thick and delicate. Frayed myocardial fibers, for sure. Her sturdy heart slammed again, again, again. No respite.

DESERT WHERE ONCE WAS OCEAN

Ask me where the water went.

Ask me why the ocean
    left behind hard evidence,
    cities of trilobites.

Ask me about echoes of lives
    lived fully
    birth to death
    millions of years ago

and now what's left. Ask me.

Mudflats crack,
    fields of pottery sherds,
    sandscapes smoothing
    shells that once housed
    scuttling hermits.

Remind me that creatures who carry
    frilled and gorgeous
    gills outside their bodies
    vanish. Remind me
    that we have no idea
    what they desired
    or dreamt.

We know only that they
    danced. In water.

Without waiting
    for anyone to ask.

THE RULE YOU DO NOT BREAK

You offer water
always in the desert,
water to anyone who walks,

water to every creature. Walk
even for one hour without water
and you begin to become desert,

every cell inside you, desert.
If you walk here
without water

your body soon
waters the desert.
Your bones walk.

—No Más Muertes

GILA MONSTER

We were taught to fear you.

Grownups said your venom
could knock us down.

I watched how you moved, calm
and thoughtful, your claws
inscribing caliche.

You never hurt
anyone I knew.

A kid would have to pry open
your jaws, put his hand
inside and say, Here,
gnaw a while.

I grew fond,
watched for you,
gentle venomous friend,
though you stayed shy
underground most days.

After-school shortcut
through the desert, ouch.
I knew better.
Jumping cactus leapt
onto my Keds
printed with the Beatles,
cholla piercing John, Paul,
George, Ringo.

A desert kid, I knew
you never reached a hand
toward what hurt.
I found a stick, flicked
spiky lobes away.
Limped home, rifled
through the junk drawer
for pliers, pulled
slow and steady
each barbed spine.

Decades it's been
since I've seen you,
friend of my youth,
yet somehow
here you are,
you've managed
three steps up
onto the porch,
tiny bellows
of your lungs
lifting your sides
with shallow breaths.

Beads black and dull orange
bubble your back.
Along both sides
where your skin turns tender,
you drag cholla,
stickers sunk deep.

We place in front of you
a gray basin
so you can't harm
yourself trying to
evade us.

With long
kitchen tongs, we pull
steady and slow
each chunk of cholla,
each spine left behind.

You hunker down
in shadows, stay so still
I fear for you.

When I stop watching,
you find your way

back into dusk.

GIVE AND TAKE

How care giving
and care taking
swirl

together, an estuary—
verge rich
with life

rising, each being
feeding on
then feeding—

from many endings

this beginning.

RED SKY

List
everything
you've lost.

Ars poetica
of heartbreak.
What's possible

to replace. What
never is. The sky's
memory, smoke.

Say a wall of flame sears
inside your eyelids every time
you close them.

What wish
Floats on streams of ash?
What sky remains?

In the waiting room
on the never-off TV
a river of poor people

draws near the line.
The talking head's
scarlet lips say

officials can process
only a trickle each day.
Thousands gather.
Next to me, a woman
with a fistula mature and swollen,
woman with her upper arm

Saran-wrapped, woman
with a beatific smile, says, "Why
process them? Just send them back."

                                           ⌒

Say a girl knows early.
Knows as a doctor
she wants to improve

world health. Say this girl
hears along the way
what girls can't do.

Say she laughs.
Say she prepares herself
to laugh a lot.

                                           ⌒

Say this season
coyotes sleek and shiny
gorge—plenty of rabbits.

Sure-footed
javelina brush by
creosote's tiny

yellow blooms,
nip new paddles
of prickly pear.

In their burrows,
whiptail lizards,
shedding rattlers,

scholarly & deliberate
Gila monsters repose,
patient as earth.

SAGUARO, HARDSHIP

Used to scant rains, saguaro
never complain

about thirst. They just suffer.
During the world's sickness,

summer rains
never came.

Saguaro grew
thin. White coronas,

bright yellow centers.
May Day crowns

adorn each arm.
Until this year.

Distressed, saguaro
sent buds

far down, spattering.
Blossoms, alive one day,

scattered. Fruits
swelled, burst—

split open
in ruby glory, spilling

tiny black waterfalls
of seed. Feasts

for cactus wrens,
mourning doves,

roadrunners,
Gambel's quail—

red flesh, ebony tears.
During the Civil War,

during the battle
of Picacho Peak,

April 1862,
this lopsided saguaro

bloomed. Back then
it had three arms

on one side. Now
it has five on that side,

one stub on the other.
One stub alone,

a girl bent over her book.
Still here,

still here.
Still thirsty.

HISTORY

Back from college, I dig out
a cardboard suitcase crammed
with old albums, photos held
by adhesive corners to thick black
crumbling pages.

In one, my grandfather loops his arm around the neck
of a dark-eyed beauty, black hair the sleek bob
favored by flappers.
Her eyes, his eyes, feral.

In another, his sweetheart
cradles an agitated goose,
its strange neck curvy,
sensuous across her breasts.

The captions, elegantly penned
(perfect penmanship) in white ink, spell out
Olga and John. "Who's Olga?" I ask.

Startled up from his newspaper, Grandpa's eyes dart.

In one breath, he's at the edge of a field,
ripe hard durum
from his toes to the horizon,
combine and crew not far off.
He hasn't been home,
hasn't slept or washed. Sweat
stiffens his skin, his
and hers, two sweats plus her sweet wet
and his. Their smells together. The tenderness left
from more and more and more and more.

He knows his father will work him extra hard
from can to can't
and more in the barn.
He knows his mother
will pack extra homemade
bread with homemade butter
in his lunch bucket,
a tart apple, a hardboiled egg.

Olga. Olga. Olga.
A biplane soars overhead. His chin lifts
and he follows it
through scattered clouds,
dream flying.
He has no way to know

that he will sign on to rig planes at an airfield out of town.
That while he's away she will dance.
That by the time Olga sashays back his way,
Harriet's almost showing.

He lowers his paper, his eyes steadfast blue.
"Your grandmother is the finest wife a man could want," he says.
And that's the end of that.

My grandmother, Harriet, who flinches
from his rowdy hugs, tilts her head,
glides her lips toward grace.

WORDS IN EVERY CELL

Beneath towering mango trees we stopped, Eva and I, stopped our walk and held each other, sobs surging through us like surf breaking. Breaking new trail, one step, another, toward and into what we could not yet know. Know this. This one hour we walked. Walked and held one another. Another sip of good company, of calm. Calm now, our voices as we turn new leaves, Eva's still-forming lines alive. Alive, my voice giving voice to Eva's words, reading to her her own prayer-poems. Prayer-poems we breathed into the breeze. Breezes carried them over the island, across the ocean named for peace. Peace, yes, and rough water. Water in all her stories. Stories of water, broken. Broken women, two women who gave birth only to words. Words in every cell of us, healthy or rogue, words around, above, beneath.

ACCOMPANIED

Thousands before me breathed
each breath that fills my lungs.

The named ones, the ones a handful
of generations back whose names

blew off in a dust storm.
A long-ago grandfather

kept on his workbench
wooden lasts in graduated sizes,

the left identical to the right
until the farmer trod

broken sod long enough
for each shoe to claim its shape.

The great-great-aunt who never
married, preferring to love

the man her mother disdained
the man who went back

to the old country
without she thought

a thought
of her. Her mother

on her deathbed
handed over

the massive sheaf of letters
she'd intercepted and kept,

daily letters for years and years.
Which the greater cruelty—

to withhold his missives
or far too late

pass them along? The mother
wanted her daughter

to stay, to care for her
(as she did) in her dotage.

That daughter claimed
her niece, my grandmother,

as her own, aimed her love
sideways. I too claim

as my child children
of my heart though not

my womb.
We are not the first.

Thousands of generations
contributed to our making,

though a few centuries
will erase our faces, our names

leaving fossils, bones, petroglyphs
spiraling over stones

and our laughter rising,
our bright eyes shining

our strange humor
and deepest sorrow

lingering in the lives
of ones far beyond us

who sense now and then
in a turn of phrase,

a quick glance
an odd knowing

that they carry
some particle of us.

DANCING WITH AZIZ

in honor of Aziz Shihab

At Ivory Jack's saloon just north of Fairbanks, Alaska,
I danced with Aziz, whose hips offered grace
to anyone who needed some.

He had the skills of a journalist
and the soul of a best friend, so before
I knew it I told him my life

as he told me his
and we were just-met lifelong
friends. His rascal eyes

saw every chance
for laughter, eyes curious
about army guys, bushy

unbathed cabin guys,
tough woman geologists just in
from the field, even

the regular who's held down
the same stool for decades—
Aziz cherished all their stories.

So I cherished his, when he told
of returning to his home
in Jerusalem, decades after

his family was forced out
at gunpoint. When it was safe
to return, new people in their family

home said it had been abandoned.
A school now, young ones studying
Talmud, sacred texts.

The woman in reception
asked, "Perhaps you'd like
to make a donation?"

And Aziz, with a smile
filled with grace and sorrow, said,
"I believe I already have."

ELECTRICITY

for David L. Hamilton

When my cousin calls from Topanga and I flail but fail
to reach my phone in time
and he's laughing into voicemail
when I interrupt him
to confess that I'm slow, he jokes

Wonder what the stats are on that? How many
people die trying to get to their phones? Trip
and impale themselves, slip
and whack their skulls, tip and crash
their just-washed cars?

He relates the latest
on his wife's surgery and radiation, and we
compare notes with my
surgery and radiation.
I ask about their brilliant

daughter, a woman now, excited
to act in Shakespeare's plays
next year in London. We jaw
about Joe's planes and his plans
to fly again after

a long time grounded. Only then
does David with his gift
for the strategic release
of information and
his finely tuned

ability to build suspense
quietly slip in that next week
surgeons will once again
open his chest, will attach
to the bundle of muscles and nerves

an electrical marvel designed
to keep him chugging along, to sense
when he needs a jolt. He says
he's going to ask for
flashing lights for his nipples.

Why not searchlights? He pictures himself
at a glitzy Hollywood party
without warning dropping
his wineglass, his bare hand
shorting out the host's

sound system. Today I tell him
"Beware of white carpet"
by which I mean
take good care
in that sterile place.

Come back out
into the raucous, grubby world
where your films, your bees, your laugh, your love
make music, where the score
taking shape composes you.

ATTENDING TO THE WORLD

You look to still water to see
what goes on in the sky.

You look to the sky
to remind yourself
you can't half the time
see the stars.

You look to the stars to teach you
that some changes return
but by the time they get back
you've changed.

You look to change
chosen or endured
to reassure
the universe, alive.

You look through a microscope
to learn the cosmos.

You look through a telescope
to comprehend the whorl
of DNA in your cells.

You look to DNA
for proof
where none exists,
our parents
removed
generation by generation.

You look to kinship
to learn how to act, grandmother
spider's web
spangled with dew.

Your own face bent
in the arc of a dewdrop,
still water carving light.

UNTIL NOW

If impatience
were left

to her, she'd
chafe

at care spent
to ease her

body only,
her mind and soul

having flown.
Beloved,

friend of your youth
and decades beyond youth,

you could not imagine
wishing her

dead.
Until now.

Swift
and serene,

let it be.

KINTSUKUROI: EACH DAY

Peculiar winter—river ice should be solid
by now, the snowpack building.
But streets are clear, the river
wide open. The river testament

to the idea that water has memory,
that what we've thrown in it will surface
or sink. No matter
how mended it looks

up top, ripples
change lives underneath.
For the first time ever
human beings have seen

traces of an asteroid
in a parallel galaxy
coming apart, a disintegrating
body spiraling

around a white dwarf star.
In the constellation Virgo,
that vast neighborhood,
this heavenly being

is chewing through
planets, a solar system
we'll never visit
coming apart.

What does it mean
that the same day
we see this, researchers
hip deep in a dig

unearth two infants
buried twelve thousand
years ago, infants
with two different

mothers, two mothers
grieving, setting into earth
arrows made of antler,
chiseled points, probably food,

though the food
was long ago eaten
by other beings
buried along the Tanana.

Eva's great wish
is to fly in her broken body
home to the death
she prefers,

in her own house,
surrounded by her closest
people, music, books, close by
Kachemak Bay, in sight

of Grace Ridge, the moon
full to welcome her. Vital,
her signs—Eva's voice the ebony
butterfly holding together

a split tabletop. Eva's
spirit a river
of kintsukuroi,
golden waterway

tracing a hurt vessel,
vessel recognized
as more beautiful
for having been broken.

BEYOND

Beyond the horizon,
light. Light not yet visible.
Visible light from stars long dead
lead us, we who
need direction, need help.
Help arrives each morning.
Morning itself a chance.
Chance, that game.
That game we devise,
pretending fate or destiny or Lutheran
predestination really
matter. Matters in our own minds,
our own hands. Hands that
shape meals, days, clay.
Clay dug from our home,
this earth, clay we crave
and swallow, clay
taking shapes of vessel
after vessel, empty,
left with respect
in the woods, left
to return to earth, beyond.

GIFTS WE CANNOT KEEP

i.m. Eva Saulitis

At the Old Kona airport,
past soccer fields and
abandoned hangars,

cracked asphalt spreads—
taxiways for miles
parallel the Pacific.

We had just come from
Body Flow, a class that,
in your words, "Kicked my ass."

By then, though, you'd caught
a second wind.
You wanted a run.

I have never wanted a run.
We did not yet know
what coursed again inside you.

You took off, gazelle in grubby
gym clothes. I clambered up
onto lava rocks

to watch the surf—
white foam turned spume
over jagged black.

Your study animals, orcas,
white and black, far from here,
gorged on seals and porpoises.

You knew already that
after the spill you were witnessing
their last days, listening

underwater for the language
spoken only by this pod,
pod that after the spill

did not make babies.
You saved your breath
for prayers in wind,

for poems and songs
and long hours glassing the water.
We had no way then

to know that they were back,
the cells that could not control
themselves, those cells.

You ran beyond where I could see.
I faced vast waters.
One moment calm, then

the ocean explodes—
barnacle-crusted humpback
full body breach

splashes me, wild eye
huge and watching—
whale pausing like Baryshnikov

in rarified air—
the great gift
of all we cannot know

laid out
before us, broken
as asphalt,

mended
as water
mends, then mends again.

LONG MARRIED

for Scott Kiefer and Sherry Simpson

Since your teens, you loved
one other, set out
feeders for hummingbirds by the dozen,

fought wildfires
in scrub brush,
in your marriage,

roasted green chilies,
made music, talked
endlessly, the conversation

a life you
made together,
your home, the one

neither of you could have made
alone, shared dogs
beloved beyond measure,

shared the high drama
of every day,
arguments

you weren't sure
you'd survive
but you did,

celebrated
private jokes
intimate as

bedcovers,
so the earth shifts
this morning

in hospice
when you lean to kiss her
and whisper

to her fierce rugged heart
thank you, hush
now, you've done all you could.

TRAVELING BESIDE WATER

thinking of Margo Klass

Nearly an hour and a half
Corea to Bangor

knowing that this
is the heartbreaking

day. Today.
Surrounded

by love
she helps

her beloved
slip

into spirit.
And after,

an hour and a half
beside water

Bangor to Corea
without.

QUESTIONS WITHOUT ANSWERS

i.m. Frank Soos

What shape this time
what shape for *this* grief

to carve out inside us,
grief that lives

deep within
grief that takes up

room we can't spare
room we still need

for loving
you, who

could not help
leaving us

leaving worn shoes
on the porch

leaving upside down
your tea mug

leaving upside down
the world

shattered
bright shards

scattered
shards we piece

together
best we can

the world
doesn't stop

though some part of it
should

some part of this world
should offer

shelter
while we cry

while we try
to shape

the wild
life left to us

into a life
worthy

of you.

FOLLOWING THE GRAIN

Curl of ash
leading on
the carver's gouge—

all that's left
of us, relief
and kindling.

(after watching Ron Senungetuk's hands at work)

A BOY I KNOW

for Levi Goodan

Opens and opens the world—
each shell at the beach
a story, a house,

a friend still living
but moved away
husk echoing

into his ear
whispers, secrets
from under waves

rollicking toward him,
this boy tells
his mother

*Art is everywhere
and everything . . .*
Boy whose heart

blesses this earth
with a beat
all its own, heart

that invites others in—
those who love him, yes,
plus teams of those

who want hearts
of children
to work better,

those who try hard
to mend hearts
mysterious and vulnerable,

graceful heart that refuses
to explain itself
in any language we know.

ZUILL BAILEY AND A 1693 MATTEO GOFFRILLER CELLO

Prelude: black leather piano bench gleams softly in a single spotlight. In the background, organ pipes stagger toward heaven.

Black shirt, black jacket, black hair—the cellist strides across the stage. Slight nod and he's seated, his instrument settled, caressed. His eyes close as his bow draws out the first notes of Bach's first suite, the notes of creation, solo for the sun's first shining, genesis. In the beginning was the sound.

We've come to hear Zuill Bailey play Bach's suites for solo cello. All of them. On one evening. Played by one cellist. This is not done. Athletic, audacious, ambitious. Gorgeous.

We've come to hear him play a cello crafted when Bach was six years old, a cello Bach probably heard, a cello whose sound Bach might have had in mind. This cello carries an ornament, a rose still visible if you look sideways under the fingerboard. Three hundred years ago, the fingerboard didn't come down so far onto the body. Players didn't have to reach around for high notes. Nobody expected high notes from them.

The cellist's not playing the repeats tonight, and who could blame him? He dances us through each suite's sturdy allemande, each suite's svelte and arrogant courante, each suite's sultry forbidden sarabande. Menuet, bourée, gavotte, gigue.

Suite No. 3 in C Major—anything is possible! The same shaped wood terrifies and soothes—the player's passion brash and reckless one moment, exquisitely quiet and courageous the next. The low notes. The low notes—the center of the earth, molten.

These strings, these strands of horsehair, this one man's hands tuned for a lifetime to these cascades of sound. They lift us. The sky opens, an aurora of music over golden hills.

E-Flat Major, Suite No. 4—Bach goes crazy, tries to hurt people. The cellist tells us, flexing his left hand, flexing, that when his hand cramps it's a ginger root. When he stretches in odd contortions, yes, I see it—tangled nubs of twisted fibers, fingers worn to nubs. Quavers.

Suite No. 6 in D Major—This is the suite cellists hate to perform. It's so easy to mangle, so hard to stretch, so difficult to scuttle so far up and down. Zuill Bailey says most players approach it like gunslingers—watch out! Once he was startled to see a buoyant cellist take the stage. Relaxed, his playing looked blissful, serene. Scent of sweet peas beside a cool stream.

Is he that much better than the rest of us? Does he somehow not know how hard this piece is? Zuill Bailey whispers to his cellist friend. The friend says, look closer. He's playing a cello piccolo. Of course. Five strings instead of four. Smaller body. No need to stretch—the piece was composed for this instrument, which didn't survive in the contemporary orchestra. Cellists who play it on modern instruments stretch like gymnasts, Olympian.

After the standing ovation, Zuill Bailey offers as an encore Bach's Suite No. 1, the piece he plays every morning, every night. That's the way he makes sure all is right in his world. His bow sails, glides. His venerable cello breathes for us. His body brings out of strings and wood all human desire, all exuberance, all grief, all curiosity, all wonder. The last vibration stills. He lifts the bow delicately, his eyes still closed. Then the bow points to the sky, the cellist lifts his face into light.

Inside us now, the sound. The sound.

EATING FROM THE CARVER'S HAND

Long before this block of alabaster
arrived in Joe Senungetuk's hands,

he flew over a place he'd never been.
Lightning from below

lit the tops of clouds, grace
arriving as it must—in a flash

that can kill or amaze
or show us our way.

Gray-edged thunderhead
of rock Joe shaped

into an ocean, each swirl
full of plankton, salt,

each crest a held breath
released, spume and foam

luring us back—the depths
our first home.

GATES OF THE ARCTIC

When we could fly,
we packed more than we needed
into the Widgeon,

pushed up a cylinder
to sample av gas—
no water, good.

We had information Juliet,
warnings of other migrants
sharing the sky.

We lifted off the ski strip,
propwash skittering
gravel and dust.

This is not a day
we could die.
Turbid waters of the Tanana

we floated over,
over gravel bars and sloughs
marshes and fens.

Banked slowly over the flats,
flew north following paths
of sandhill cranes and Canada geese,

over nests relined and clutches warmed
by belly skin deliberately
unfeathered. Hillsides scoured by wildfire

now riots of fireweed,
delicate tips of new willow
red, swelling.

The hardest parts of this earth
haven't worn away. Yet.
The tors face up

to every force
that would tear them down.
The Yukon bends,

mighty toward the Bering Sea.
The Arctic Circle
no boundary we can see.

Into the Arrigetch,
no place to set down,
peaks sharp as panes just broken.

Wind shears jagged,
invisible, slice our wings,
guillotines honed

to chop us out of sky.
If we go down,
someone would look, but

they might not find
what's left of us
until long after

no trace is left.
No sky so clear
as this serrated

infinite. No one can
stay here long.
We have this time,

this time only.
Wings turn toward
a still center

full of driftwood
and tannins, scatter
three loons

as our belly
slips onto the surface,
the Widgeon

plowing a water furrow,
splash sides rising
in rooster tails,

our wake
dramatic this instant
invisible the next.

ALIVE

How many centuries
for ivory to mellow,
fossil carved
two thousand years ago
by hands these colors—
walrus hide, seal oil,
driftwood, smoke.

As the carver spoke
to the stone, this woman
emerged, heavy-eyed,
bemused, the corner
of her mouth tipped up
as if she knew
a secret

she's still not telling.
What wore away
her baby's face?
Water maybe or wind
or the constant caress
of weather-worn
fingers in a shaman's pouch.

How odd now
to regard her
on display,
spot-lit,
even the shadows
she casts
compelling.

Hello across centuries, woman
of Okvik. Thank you, carver
from Panuk Island.
Though your bones and the bones
of your babies turned
fossils long before
anyone here blinked,

you live.

ABOUT THE AUTHOR

Peggy Shumaker is the daughter of two deserts—the Sonoran desert around Tucson and the subarctic desert of Interior Alaska. She was honored by the Rasmuson Foundation as its Distinguished Artist, served as Alaska State Writer Laureate, and received a poetry fellowship from the National Endowment for the Arts. She is the author of ten books of poetry, including *Cairn*, her new and selected. Her lyrical memoir is *Just Breathe Normally*. Professor emerita from University of Alaska Fairbanks, Shumaker taught in the Rainier Writing Workshop MFA at Pacific Lutheran University. She serves on the Advisory Board for the Raz-Shumaker *Prairie Schooner* Book Prizes and for the Kachemak Bay Writers Conference. Shumaker is editor of the Boreal Books series (an imprint of Red Hen Press), editor of the Alaska Literary Series at University of Alaska Press, and contributing editor for *Alaska Quarterly Review*.

www.ingramcontent.com/pod-product-compliance
Lightning Source LLC
Jackson TN
JSHW081239220125
77584JS00001B/2